Planet Mars

ANN O. SQUIRE

Children's Press®
An Imprint of Scholastic Inc.
New York   Toronto   London   Auckland   Sydney
Mexico City   New Delhi   Hong Kong
Danbury, Connecticut

Content Consultant
Bryan C. Dunne
Assistant Chair, Assistant Professor, Department of Astronomy
University of Illinois at Urbana–Champaign
Urbana, Illinois

Library of Congress Cataloging-in-Publication Data
Squire, Ann.
 Mars / Ann O. Squire.
 pages cm. — (A true book)
 Audience: Grade 4 to 6.
 Includes bibliographical references and index.
 ISBN 978-0-531-21152-6 (lib. bdg.) — ISBN 978-0-531-25358-8 (paperback)
 1. Mars (Planet)—Juvenile literature. I. Title.
 QB641.S677 2014
 523.43—dc23   2013019580

© 2014 Scholastic Inc.

All rights reserved. Published in 2014 by Children's Press, an imprint of Scholastic Inc.
Printed in China 62
SCHOLASTIC, CHILDREN'S PRESS, A TRUE BOOK™, and associated logos are trademarks and/or registered trademarks of Scholastic Inc.

1 2 3 4 5 6 7 8 9 10 R 23 22 21 20 19 18 17 16 15 14

Front cover: The *Opportunity* rover on Mars

Back cover: Mars, as seen from its moon Deimos

Find the Truth!

Everything you are about to read is true *except* for one of the sentences on this page.

Which one is **TRUE**?

T or F A spacecraft can make the trip to Mars in three weeks.

T or F Mars is colder and darker than Earth.

Find the answers in this book.

3

Contents

← Christiaan Huygens was the first astronomer to estimate the length of Mars's day.

Our solar system contains eight planets and several other objects orbiting the sun.

Martian Invasions

Mars shines above houses in northern Spain in 2003.

CHAPTER 1

The Red Planet

On August 27, 2003, sky watchers on Earth got a rare treat. The **planet** Mars appeared as a bright light in the night sky. On that date, Mars and Earth were closer to each other than they had been in 50,000 years. Mars was only about 34,646,000 miles (55,757,000 kilometers) away. It was easy to see Mars's rusty red color even without a telescope.

Galileo Galilei was the first to use a telescope to study other planets.

Mars's Place in the Solar System

Mars is one of the eight planets in our solar system. It is the fourth planet from the sun. Mars is **terrestrial**, made up mostly of rock and metal. The other terrestrial planets are Mercury, Venus, and Earth. Along with Mars, these planets are closest to the sun and are among the solar system's smallest planets. The outer planets are Jupiter, Saturn, Uranus, and Neptune. They are mostly gas and liquids and are much larger than the terrestrial planets.

If Mars were the size of a marble, Jupiter would be the size of a basketball.

Mercury

Venus

Earth

Mars

Jupiter

Saturn

Uranus

Neptune

Because Mars is smaller and less dense than Earth, it has less gravity. A person would feel lighter on Mars than he or she does on Earth.

A Small Planet

Mars is the second-smallest planet in our solar system, after Mercury. If you sliced Mars in half and measured across the widest point, it would measure 4,220 miles (6,791 km). Earth is almost twice as wide, at 7,926 miles (12,756 km). This is similar to the difference between a tangerine and an orange. Mars is also less **dense** than Earth is, having only one-ninth of Earth's mass.

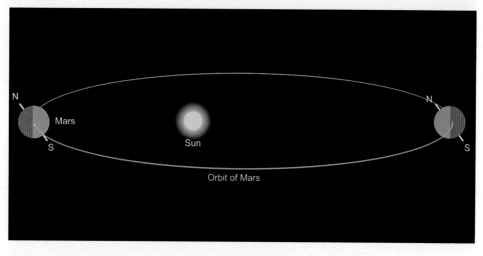

Mars is the farthest terrestrial planet from the sun.

Distance From the Sun

Mars **orbits** the sun at an average distance of 141,700,000 miles (228,044,000 km). But the distance at any given time is always changing. This is because Mars's orbit is an **ellipse,** or oval. The point on the ellipse at which Mars is farthest from the sun is called the aphelion. Mars's aphelion is 154,900,000 miles (249,287,000 km) from the sun. The point where Mars is closest is the perihelion. There, Mars is 128,400,000 miles (206,640,000 km) from the sun.

Distance From Earth

The distance between Earth and Mars is constantly changing. Both planets follow elliptical orbits. They are also generally at different places in their orbits around the sun. Sometimes Earth and Mars are on opposite sides of the sun. Then the distance between them is huge. It can be as much as 249,000,000 miles (400,727,000 km). When they are on the same side of the sun, they come much closer, as they did in August 2003.

This diagram shows the orbits of the inner planets, as well as portions of Jupiter's and Saturn's orbits.

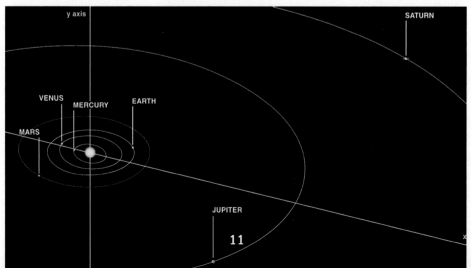

11

A Longer Day

Like all other planets in our solar system, Mars rotates on its **axis**. This rotation creates a day on the planet. A day is the average time between one sunrise to the next sunrise. On Earth, a day is 24 hours long. Mars takes just a bit more time to rotate on its axis. This makes the Martian day slightly longer. There, a day lasts 24 hours, 39 minutes, and 23 seconds.

A day on Mars is almost the same length as a day on Earth.

Scientists controlling the robotic rovers on Mars live on Martian time, with its slightly longer day.

Mars orbits the sun at about 15 miles (24 km) per second.

A Much Longer Year

The length of time it takes a planet to make one trip around the sun is known as a year. Planets close to the sun make this trip quickly. Their orbits are relatively small. The planets also move faster. Planets farther from the sun have longer distances to travel. These planets move more slowly. Earth makes one orbit about every 365 days. Mars is farther from the sun, so its orbit takes longer. Its year is nearly 669 Martian days (687 Earth days) long.

Mars is known for its dust storms, which cloud portions of the planet in this photograph. This can most easily be seen around the north pole (top).

CHAPTER 2

Geography and Climate

If you spot Mars in the night sky, the first thing you will notice is its red color. This comes from iron oxide dust that covers the planet's surface. You have probably seen iron oxide many times. It is rust! Strong winds on Mars pick up the rusty dust and carry it into the **atmosphere**. The dust reflects sunlight, giving Mars a reddish glow.

Sometimes dust storms surround all of Mars with thick, red dust.

The Surface of Mars

You will see more of Mars if you look through a telescope. Then you'll see some striking similarities between Mars and Earth. Like our planet, Mars has ice caps at its north and south poles. There are also volcanoes, canyons, mountains, and channels that resemble dry riverbeds. These channels, along with large amounts of underground ice, hint that the red planet may once have been a much wetter place. Today, there is no evidence of liquid water on Mars.

The canyon Valles Marineris forms a deep scar across the surface of Mars.

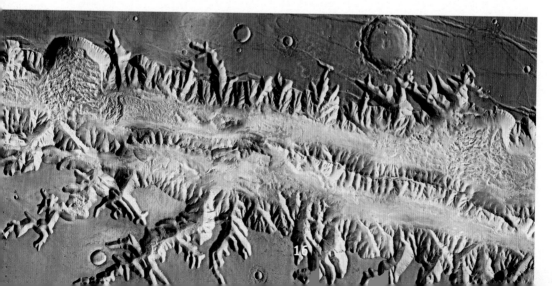

16

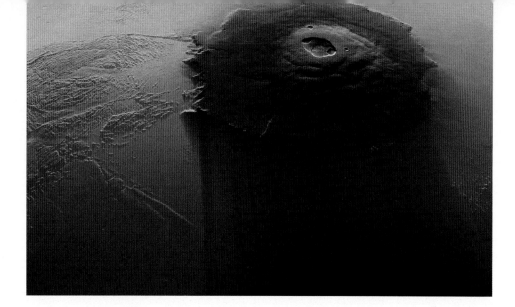

The base of Olympus Mons could cover all of New Mexico.

Mountains and Canyons

Mars is home to the tallest mountain in the solar system. Olympus Mons is an extinct volcano that stands 16 miles (25.7 km) high. This is three times as tall as Mount Everest in Nepal. Mars also boasts the solar system's deepest canyon. Valles Marineris is up to 6.2 miles (10 km) deep and 2,485 miles (4,000 km) long. It is nearly four times as deep and 10 times as long as Arizona's Grand Canyon.

Mars's ice caps grow and shrink with the seasons, just like Earth's do.

Polar Ice Caps

Astronomers have observed that Mars's ice caps grow during winter. How can this be, if Mars has no liquid water today? The bottom, unchanging layers of the ice caps are frozen water. However, the top, seasonal layers are frozen carbon dioxide (CO_2), or dry ice. Mars's atmosphere is mostly CO_2 gas. As the weather cools, the gas solidifies into ice. When summer comes, the ice caps shrink as the dry ice vaporizes into CO_2 gas.

Seasons on Mars

Like Earth, Mars is tilted on its axis. This tilt gives both planets their four seasons. When it is summer in Mars's northern **hemisphere**, it is winter in the south. The seasons work the same way on Earth. Because the Martian year is longer than Earth's year, each season is about twice as long as Earth's. Winters on Mars are severely cold. With very little water in Mars's atmosphere, it does not snow. Summers are less cold, but it's hardly beach weather.

Different hemispheres are tilted toward the sun at different points in Mars's orbit.

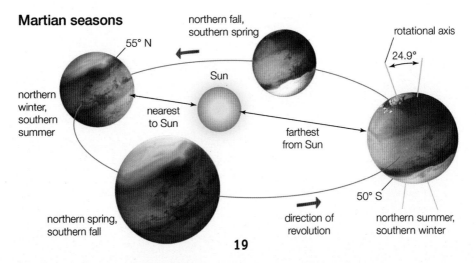

Martian seasons

northern fall, southern spring

rotational axis

55° N

24.9°

Sun

northern winter, southern summer

nearest to Sun

farthest from Sun

northern spring, southern fall

direction of revolution

50° S

northern summer, southern winter

Life on Mars?

Mars seems like Earth in so many ways. People have long wondered if the red planet is capable of supporting life. For a number of reasons, the answer is probably not today. The environment on Mars is harsh and usually quite cold. There is no liquid water on the surface, and massive storms often fill the air with dust. The air is also too thin—there is not enough oxygen for humans to breathe.

Mars would not be able to support life as we know it on Earth.

A thin line of atmosphere can be seen above Mars's edge (top).

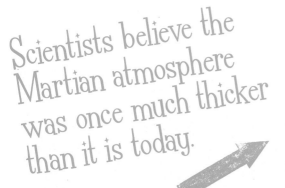

Scientists believe the Martian atmosphere was once much thicker than it is today.

Thin Atmosphere

Earth's atmosphere shields our planet from the sun's harmful rays during the day. It also holds in heat at night. Because of this, temperatures on Earth do not change much during the course of a day. Mars's atmosphere is too thin to repel the sun's harmful **ultraviolet radiation**. Temperatures on Mars can vary widely, too. Summer temperatures near the equator can reach 95 degrees Fahrenheit (35 degrees Celsius) in the daytime. They drop to −166°F (−110°C) on winter nights!

The comparatively small sun sinks below the horizon at sunset on Mars.

A Cold, Dim Planet

The average temperature on Mars is around −80°F (−62°C). This is much colder than the temperature on Earth. Mars is about one and a half times farther from the sun than Earth is. It gets less than half as much sunlight. So even a clear, sunny day on Mars would look dim to us. On Mars, the sun also appears smaller than the way we see it from Earth.

Colonizing Mars

Some people believe it is possible for humans to live permanently on Mars. A Dutch group named Mars One has already begun planning the first human colony on Mars. The group hopes to begin sending supplies to Mars in 2016. They would be followed by robotic rovers that would construct places to live. The first human crew would arrive in 2023.

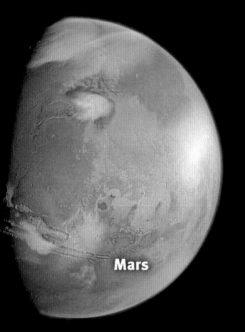

Phobos

Deimos

Mars

In this illustratioin, Deimos appears much larger than Phobos. This is because Deimos is much closer to the viewer than Phobos is.

CHAPTER 3

The Moons of Mars

Mars has two small moons: Phobos and Deimos. Compared to our moon, these moons are tiny. Phobos measures only 13.8 miles (22.2 km) across. Deimos is even smaller, at 7.8 miles (12.6 km) across. Both Phobos and Deimos are lumpy and irregular in shape. They are also covered with rocks and craters. Some astronomers believe that the moons are actually **asteroids** that have been captured by Mars's gravitational pull.

Mars is the only terrestrial planet in our solar system with more than one moon.

A Lunar Discovery

Experts once thought that Mars had no moons. That's because the moons were too small and too close to the planet to be noticed. But in 1877, American astronomer Asaph Hall was studying Mars through a telescope at the U.S. Naval **Observatory** in Washington, D.C. He spotted

Deimos on August 12 and Phobos six days later. Hall named the moons after the twin sons of Ares, the Greek god of war. The Romans knew Ares as Mars.

Asaph Hall studied mathematics and geometry before his work in astronomy.

Phobos travels at about twice the speed of Earth's moon.

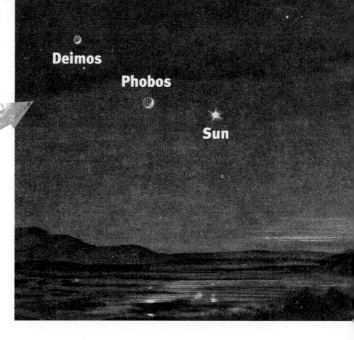

Deimos

Phobos

Sun

This illustration shows how Phobos and Deimos might look in Mars's evening sky.

Moons in Orbit

Phobos orbits only about 3,700 miles (5,955 km) above the surface of Mars. In comparison, our moon is 238,900 miles (384,470 km) from Earth. Because Phobos is so close, it circles Mars in about seven hours. Deimos is more than 14,000 miles (22,531 km) from Mars. It takes 30 hours to complete one orbit. On Mars, Deimos would appear as a tiny object in the sky because of its small size and distance from the planet.

Mars's gravity is pulling Phobos in.

A Collision Course

The orbits of both Phobos and Deimos are changing. Phobos, already near the Martian surface, is getting a tiny bit closer every day. This moon is spiraling inward toward Mars at the rate of 6 feet (1.8 meters) per century. Astronomers estimate that in about 50 million years, it will either crash into Mars or break up into a ring of rocks and debris.

An Escaping Moon

Deimos is almost four times farther from the surface of Mars than Phobos is. The pull of Mars's gravity on this small moon is much weaker. With less gravity to keep it in the planet's orbit, Deimos is spiraling slowly away from Mars. In millions of years, Deimos may escape Mars's orbit altogether and float off into space.

These photos of Deimos show its relatively smooth, dusty surface dotted with craters.

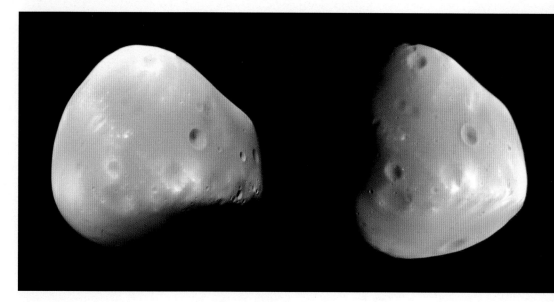

CHAPTER 4

Early Views of Mars

The most striking aspect of Mars is its strong red color. The ancient Egyptians referred to Mars as Har Decher, "the red one." Many cultures, including Sumerian, Greek, and Roman, associated this red planet with war and bloodshed. It has had many names. The one we use today is Mars, named after the Roman god of war.

The month of March is also named after the Roman god Mars.

First Observations

It is impossible to say who actually "discovered" Mars. It is so bright and so easily spotted in the night sky that people have observed and studied it for thousands of years. By 1500 BCE, Egyptian astronomers were studying Mars and its motion in

relation to other objects in the night sky. In the fourth century BCE, the Greek philosopher Aristotle noticed that Mars sometimes disappeared behind our moon. This showed that Mars is more distant from Earth than the moon.

Early astronomers noticed that Mars and other planets moved differently from other objects in the night sky.

Christiaan Huygens made improvements to the telescope, which helped him in his observations.

Mars Through a Telescope

In 1609, Italian astronomer and physicist Galileo Galilei was the first to observe Mars through an early "spyglass," or telescope. Astronomers learned more about the red planet as telescopes improved. Later in the 1600s, Dutch astronomer Christiaan Huygens estimated the size of Mars. He also made drawings of Mars's geographic features and polar ice caps. Huygens later published a book called *Cosmotheoros*. In it, he speculates about the possibility of life on Mars.

The more people looked, the more similarities they saw between Earth and Mars. In the late 1700s, British astronomer William Herschel wrote that the dark areas on Mars were oceans. The lighter ones were land. He believed there was life on Mars and that Martians probably lived in an environment much like ours. In the late 1800s, scientist Giovanni Schiaparelli saw straight lines on the Martian surface. He declared they were canals built by intelligent life-forms.

Timeline of Martian Exploration

1576
Danish astronomer Tycho Brahe sets up an observatory where he studies Mars and other planets.

1666
Mathematician and astronomer Giovanni Cassini determines that the Martian day is about 40 minutes longer than a day on Earth.

Canal Fever

Wealthy businessman and astronomer Percival Lowell supported Schiaparelli's claims. In 1894, Lowell built an observatory in Flagstaff, Arizona. He spent the next 15 years studying Mars. He drew maps of the canals and published his observations. As a result of his books, many people believed in the canals and thought that Mars was home to intelligent life. As bigger and better telescopes were developed, it became clear that the "canals" were mostly optical illusions.

1672

Dutch astronomer Christiaan Huygens first sees the ice cap at Mars's south pole.

1809

French astronomer Honoré Flaugergues sees yellow clouds on Mars. These are later found to be dust clouds.

1965

The *Mariner 4* spacecraft passes by Mars, sending back 21 images of the planet.

Martian Invasions

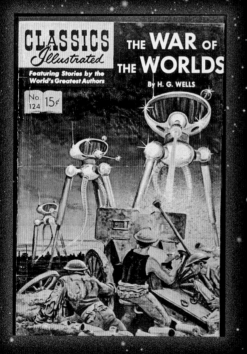

In 1898, author H. G. Wells published *The War of the Worlds*. In his book, Martians travel to Earth in metal cylinders and try to take over our planet. In the 1890s, a Martian invasion seemed possible, thanks to publications from scientists such as Schiaparelli and Lowell.

Even after experts determined that canals did not exist on Mars, the idea of Martians captured the public's imagination. In 1938, actor and filmmaker Orson Welles (right) narrated a radio program based on *The War of the Worlds*. Many frightened listeners thought the program was a newscast and that Martians really had invaded Earth.

Since then, there have been many television shows and movies about Martians coming to Earth. *My Favorite Martian*, *Mars Attacks!*, and *Mars Needs Moms* are just a few examples.

Mariner 4 approaches Mars in 1964.

CHAPTER 5

Modern Exploration of Mars

In the 1960s, scientists started trying to send unmanned spacecraft to Mars. The first few attempts were failures. Then in 1964, the United States launched *Mariner 4*. The satellite flew past Mars on July 14, 1965. Its photos showed a dry planet pockmarked with craters. *Mariner 9* went into orbit around Mars in November 1971. After waiting for a huge dust storm to pass, *Mariner 9* sent back photos of the Martian landscape and Mars's two moons.

A trip to Mars takes more than seven months!

Landing on Mars

In 1976, the National Aeronautics and Space Administration (NASA) made history. That year, two of its spacecraft, *Viking 1* and *Viking 2*, landed on the surface of Mars. The two landers collected samples from the Martian surface and conducted experiments. They also sent back photos to scientists on Earth. The experiments revealed some unexpected chemical activity in the soil near the landing sites. However, there was no evidence of life on Mars.

The *Viking* landers gave astronomers the first opportunity to take soil samples on Mars.

Finding a Launch Window

Launching a rocket takes careful planning. Launching when Mars and Earth are closest saves fuel and makes the trip as quick as possible. Also, both Earth and Mars are always moving. Engineers must calculate where Mars will be when the spacecraft reaches the planet's orbit. They then direct the rocket to that point in space. If all goes well, Mars and the spacecraft arrive at the same place at the same time.

Curiosity landed on Mars in August 2012.

Missions to Mars

Since the 1970s, the United States and other countries have launched many more spacecraft to Mars. As of 2013, the United States has two spacecraft orbiting Mars. Both are equipped with powerful cameras and are sending back detailed photos of Mars. In addition, four robotic rovers have worked on the surface of Mars. The rovers have collected and analyzed soil samples. They have also provided close-up photos of the Martian terrain. Two of the rovers are still active today.

Future Missions

The United States and other countries have ambitious plans for future explorations of Mars. The next launch will be an orbiting spacecraft designed to study the Martian atmosphere. It will help determine how the climate of Mars has changed over time. Later missions will include orbiters and land-based rovers that will study whether life could ever have existed there. In the future, there may even be manned missions to Mars. Would you want to go? ★

Manned missions to Mars will take several years to plan.

43

True Statistics

Time it would take to reach Mars from Earth by driving a car at 60 miles per hour (96.6 kph): 271 years and 221 days

Wind speed during a Martian dust storm: 60 mph. (96.6 kph)

Weight of a 100-pound (45 kg) person on Mars: 38 lb. (this would feel like 17.2 kg on Earth)

Weight of a 100-pound (45 kg) person on Phobos: 0.93 oz. (this would feel like 26.4 g on Earth)

Year when Mars will be as close to Earth as it was in 2003: 2287

Did you find the truth?

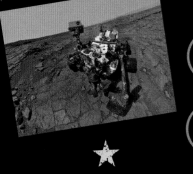

(F) A spacecraft can make the trip to Mars in three weeks.

(T) Mars is colder and darker than Earth.

Resources

Books

Carson, Mary Kay. *Far-Out Guide to Mars*. Berkeley Heights, NJ: Enslow Publishers, 2011.

Rusch, Elizabeth. *The Mighty Mars Rovers: The Incredible Adventures of* Spirit *and* Opportunity. Boston: Houghton Mifflin Books for Children, 2012.

Visit this Scholastic Web site for more information on Mars:
★ www.factsfornow.scholastic.com
Enter the keyword **Mars**

Important Words

asteroids (AS-tuh-roidz) — small, rocky objects that travel around the sun

astronomers (uh-STRAH-nuh-muhrz) — scientists who study stars, planets, and space

atmosphere (AT-muhs-feer) — the mixture of gases that surrounds a planet

axis (AK-sus) — an imaginary line through the middle of an object, around which that object spins

dense (DENS) — having a large amount of matter packed tightly together

ellipse (i-LIPS) — a flat oval shape

hemisphere (HEM-uh-sfeer) — one half of a round object, especially a planet

observatory (uhb-ZUR-vuh-tor-ee) — a special building that has telescopes or other instruments for studying the stars, planets, or weather

orbits (OR-bits) — travels in a path around something, especially a planet or the sun

planet (PLAN-it) — a large body orbiting a star

terrestrial (tuh-RES-tree-uhl) — relating to land as distinct from air or water

ultraviolet radiation (ul-truh-VYE-uh-lut ray-dee-AY-shuhn) — potentially dangerous energy with a wavelength shorter than those of visible light but longer than those of x-rays

Index

Page numbers in **bold** indicate illustrations

About the Author

Ann O. Squire is a psychologist and an animal behaviorist. Before becoming a writer, she studied the behaviors of rats, tropical fish in the Caribbean, and electric fish from central Africa. Her favorite part of being a writer is the chance to learn as much as she can about all sorts of topics. In addition to *Mars*, *Jupiter*, *Mercury*, *Neptune*, and *Saturn*, Dr. Squire has written about many different animals, from lemmings to leopards and cicadas to cheetahs. She lives in Long Island City, New York.